Happy Holidays!
Halloween

by Betsy Rathburn

BELLWETHER MEDIA
MINNEAPOLIS, MN

Blastoff! Beginners are developed by literacy experts and educators to meet the needs of early readers. These engaging informational texts support young children as they begin reading about their world. Through simple language and high frequency words paired with crisp, colorful photos, Blastoff! Beginners launch young readers into the universe of independent reading.

Sight Words in This Book

a	go	people	up
all	is	play	want
and	it	the	
are	look	they	
get	on	to	

This edition first published in 2023 by Bellwether Media, Inc.

No part of this publication may be reproduced in whole or in part without written permission of the publisher. For information regarding permission, write to Bellwether Media, Inc., Attention: Permissions Department, 6012 Blue Circle Drive, Minnetonka, MN 55343.

Library of Congress Cataloging-in-Publication Data

Names: Rathburn, Betsy, author.
Title: Halloween / by Betsy Rathburn.
Description: Minneapolis, MN : Bellwether Media, 2023. | Series: Blastoff! beginners. Happy holidays! | Includes bibliographical references and index. | Audience: Ages 4-7 | Audience: Grades K-1
Identifiers: LCCN 2022009286 (print) | LCCN 2022009287 (ebook) | ISBN 9781644876794 (library binding) | ISBN 9781648348549 (paperback) | ISBN 9781648347252 (ebook)
Subjects: LCSH: Halloween--Juvenile literature.
Classification: LCC GT4965 .R28 2023 (print) | LCC GT4965 (ebook) | DDC 394.2646--dc23/eng/20220224
LC record available at https://lccn.loc.gov/2022009286
LC ebook record available at https://lccn.loc.gov/2022009287

Text copyright © 2023 by Bellwether Media, Inc. BLASTOFF! BEGINNERS and associated logos are trademarks and/or registered trademarks of Bellwether Media, Inc.

Editor: Christina Leaf   Designer: Laura Sowers

Printed in the United States of America, North Mankato, MN.

Table of Contents

It Is Halloween!	4
A Spooky Night	6
Scary and Silly	10
Halloween Facts	22
Glossary	23
To Learn More	24
Index	24

It Is Halloween!

Trick or treat!
Kids get candy.
Happy Halloween!

A Spooky Night

Halloween is on October 31. It is a **spooky** night!

People all over the world enjoy it!

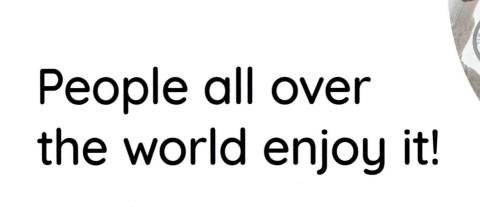

Scary and Silly

People put up webs and bats. They want a spooky look.

bats

People **carve** pumpkins. They light candles inside.

People dress up. **Costumes** are scary or silly.

People go to parties. They play games.

Kids trick or treat.
They visit houses.
They get candy!

trick or treating

People tell ghost stories. Halloween is scary and fun!

Halloween Facts

Celebrating Halloween

candy

pumpkin

costume

Halloween Activities

carve pumpkins

wear a costume

trick or treat

Glossary

carve

to cut out a certain shape

costumes

clothes worn to look like something or someone else

spooky

scary or creepy

To Learn More

ON THE WEB

FACTSURFER

Factsurfer.com gives you a safe, fun way to find more information.

1. Go to www.factsurfer.com.

2. Enter "Halloween" into the search box and click 🔍.

3. Select your book cover to see a list of related content.

Index

bats, 10
candles, 12
candy, 4, 18
carve, 12
costumes, 14, 15
dress up, 14
games, 16

ghost stories, 20
houses, 18
kids, 4, 18
night, 6
October, 6
parties, 16
pumpkins, 12
scary, 14, 20

silly, 14
spooky, 6, 10
trick or treat, 4, 18, 19
visit, 18
webs, 10, 11

The images in this book are reproduced through the courtesy of: JeniFoto, front cover; DenisNata, p. 3; FamVeld, pp. 4-5, 22 (trick or treat); Rawpixel, pp. 6-7; skynesher, pp. 8-9; AtlasStudio, p. 10; LightField Studios, pp. 10-11; Romolo Tavani, p. 12; evgenyatamanenko, pp. 12-13; Marco Govel, p. 14; 1981 Rustic Studio kan, pp. 14-15; Sean Locke Photography, p. 16; gpointstudio, pp. 16-17; Sandra Cunningham, p. 18; Rawpixelimages, pp. 18-19; Viktorcvetkovic, pp. 20-21; Sandy Morelli, p. 22; :tdub303, p. 22 (carve pumpkins); Pressmaster, p. 22 (wear a costume); Joshua Resnick, p. 23 (carve); svetlana_apo, p. 23 (costumes); Sunny studio, p. 23 (spooky).

24